Introduction

Have you ever wondered how a quilt would look if you used just a single triangle shape? It sounds like all you would get would be a boring, not-very-exciting quilt. But... quilts in One-Patch Triangle Quilts give you just a sampling of the amazing designs that can be done with... You can have Twirling Pinwheels and Hidden Stars as well as Hearts and Tulips and a Trip Around the W... -cutter techniques and full-color quilt layouts make One-Patch Triangle Quilts fun and simple to do. You w... t to make just one!

Contents

General Instructions

The Fabric

The preferred fabric for quiltmaking is 100 percent cotton fabric. It is easy to work with and will wear much better than almost any other type of fabric.

Prewashing is not necessary, but pretesting your fabric for colorfastness and shrinkage is strongly advised. Start by cutting 2"-wide strips from each fabric that you will be using. To determine whether the fabric is colorfast, immerse each strip separately into a clean bowl of extremely hot water, or hold the fabric strip under hot running water. If your fabric bleeds a great deal, all is not lost. You might be able to wash all of that fabric until all of the excess dye has washed out. Fabrics that continue to bleed after they have been washed several times should be eliminated.

To test for shrinkage, take each saturated strip and iron it dry with a hot iron, being careful not to stretch it. When the strip is completely dry, measure and compare it to your original 2"-wide strip. If all your fabric strips shrink about the same amount, then you really have no problem. When you wash your finished quilt, you may achieve the puckered look of an antique quilt. If you do not want this look, you will have to wash and dry all of the fabric before beginning so that shrinkage is no longer a problem. Use spray starch or sizing when ironing fabric to give a crisp finish.

Techniques

Rotary Cutting

Supplies

For rotary cutting, you will need a mat, acrylic ruler and a rotary cutter. There are many different brands and types of supplies on the market. Choose supplies that are comfortable for you.

Mats come in various sizes, but if you are new to rotary cutting, an 18" x 24" mat is a good choice. Be sure to keep your mat on a flat surface when not in use so that it doesn't bend. Also, avoid direct sunlight—heat will cause the mat to become warped. Bent or warped mats will decrease the accuracy of your cutting.

Acrylic rulers are a must for safe and accurate cutting. Be sure your ruler has ⅛" increment markings in both directions as well as a 45-degree marking. Either the 6" x 24" or 6" x 12" size is recommended. The larger size is long enough to use with the fabric only folded once. Using the smaller size requires that you fold the fabric twice in order to cut.

There are several different rotary cutters currently available. Read the labels to find one with features that you prefer such as type of handle, adaptability (for right- and left-handed use), safety, size and cost.

Cutting Strips

Iron fabric to remove wrinkles, then fold in half lengthwise, bringing selvages together. Fold in half again, **Fig 1**. Be sure there aren't any wrinkles in the fabric.

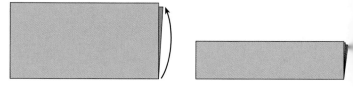

Fig 1

Square up fabric first. Place folded fabric on cutting mat with the fabric length on the right (or left for left-handers), **Fig 2**. Line up fold of fabric along one of the mat grid lines. Place acrylic ruler near cut edge, with ruler markings even with mat grid. Hold ruler firmly with left hand (right hand for left-handers), with small finger off the mat to provide extra stability. Hold rotary cutter with blade against ruler and cut away from you in one motion, **Fig 3**.

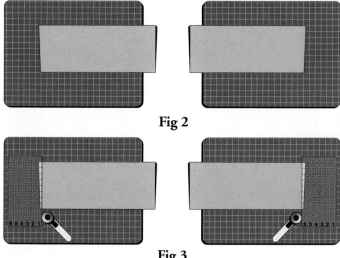

Fig 2

Fig 3

Place ruler with appropriate width line along cut edge of fabric and cut strip, **Fig 4**. Continue cutting the number of strips needed for your project.

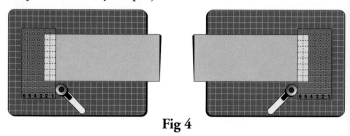

Fig 4

*Note: After cutting a few strips, check to make sure your fabric is squared up and re-square if necessary. If you don't, your strips may have a "v" in the center, **Fig 5**, causing inaccurate piecing.*

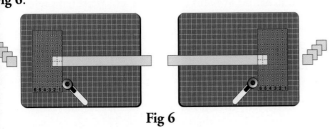

Fig. 5

Cutting Squares

Place a stack of strips (no more than four) on cutting mat; be sure strips are lined up evenly. Cut required number of squares or rectangles referring to the project instructions, **Fig 6**.

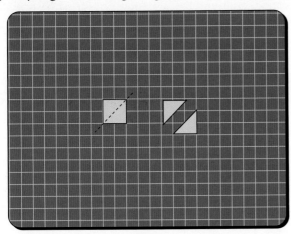

Fig 6

Half-Square Triangles

Most of the quilts require half-square triangles. Half-square triangles have their short sides on the straight grain of the fabric. This is necessary if these edges are on the outer edge of the block.

You can choose from two ways to cut and sew half-square triangles. First, cut squares the required size, then cut in half diagonally, **Fig 7**. Sew triangles together to form a square, **Fig 8**.

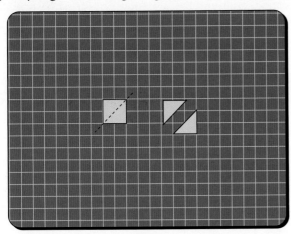

Fig 7

Fig 8

Second, cut squares the required size. Place two squares right sides together. Draw a diagonal line from corner to corner on wrong side of lighter square, **Fig 9**.

Fig 9

Sew ¼" from each side of diagonal line, **Fig 10**.

Fig 10

Cut along drawn line to get two squares, **Fig 11**; press open.

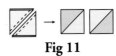

Fig 11

The second method is especially useful when many of the same triangle squares are needed for your project.

Quarter-Square Triangles

Quarter-square triangles are made by cutting a square, then cutting the square diagonally into quarters, **Fig 12**. These triangles have their longest side on the straight grain of the fabric.

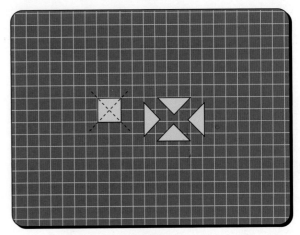

Fig 12

Chain Piecing

For faster and more efficient sewing, use chain piecing when there are several of the same shapes to sew. For example, if you have several half-square triangles to sew together, place two triangles right sides together; sew along longest edge, **Fig 13**. Without lifting the presser foot or cutting the thread, sew next pair. Continue sewing pairs of triangles until all are sewn, **Fig 14**. Press seams toward darker fabric. Pairs can be cut apart when needed.

Fig 13

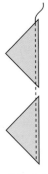

Fig 14

Making the Quilt

Sewing the Quilt Top

There are two methods of sewing the quilt top together. Use the method with which you feel most comfortable.

First, following the quilt layout, sew triangles together to form squares; sew squares together in rows. After sewing, press seams for rows in alternate directions to allow for easier piecing. Sew rows together, making sure to match seams.

Second, following quilt layout, sew squares together in pairs, then sew pairs together. Continue sewing in pairs until quilt top is complete, **Fig 15**.

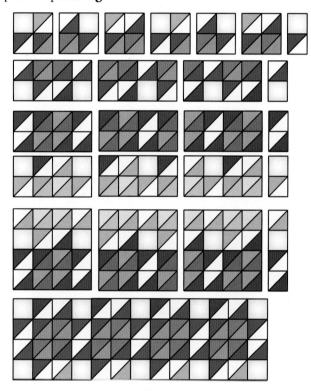

Fig 15

Adding Borders

To add borders, measure quilt top lengthwise; cut two border strips to that length and sew to sides of quilt. Measure quilt top crosswise, including borders just added and cut two border strips to that length. Sew to top and bottom of quilt top. Repeat for any additional borders. Press quilt top carefully.

Finishing Your Quilt

Marking the Quilt Top

Decide how you would like to quilt your quilt. If you are quilting in the ditch of the seams (the space right in the seam), marking is not necessary. If you are quilting around shapes (stars, flowers, etc.), you may not need to mark the lines if you feel that you can accurately gauge the quilting lines as you work. Any other quilting will need to be marked.

Before marking on your quilt top, be sure to test any marking material to make sure it will wash out of your fabric. Mark all quilting lines on the right side of the fabric. For marking,

use a hard-lead pencil, chalk or other special quilt-marking materials. If you quilt right on the marked lines, they will no show. If they do show, follow manufacturer's directions to remove any marks.

A word of caution: Marking lines which are intended to disappear after quilting—either by exposure to air or water—may become permanent when set with a hot iron. Therefore, don't iron your quilt top after you have marked your quilting pattern.

Attaching the Batting & Backing

There are many types of batting on the market. Choosing your batting will depend on how you will use your quilt, if you are machine or hand quilting or just personal preference. If you are making a wall hanging, a thin cotton batting is best. If you are machine quilting, use a thin cotton or cotton/polyester blend. Use thick polyester batting if you are tying a quilt. The new fusible battings are wonderful. They eliminate the need for basting.

Use 100 percent cotton fabric for the backing of your quilt. If your quilt is larger than the 42"- to 44"-wide fabrics, you will have to piece the backing or get the 90"- or 108"-wide fabrics that are also available.

Cut backing and batting about 2" larger on all sides than the quilt top. Place backing wrong side up on a flat surface, then smooth out batting on top. Center the quilt top right side up on the batting.

The layers of the quilt must now be held together before quilting. There are several methods: thread basting, safety-pin basting, quilt-gun basting, spray or heat-set basting and fusible iron-on batting.

Thread basting—Baste with long stitches, starting in the center and sewing toward edges in a number of diagonal lines.

Safety-pin basting—Pin through all layers at once, starting from center and working toward edges. Place pins no more than 4" apart, thinking of your quilt plan as you work to make certain pins avoid prospective quilting lines.

Quilt-gun basting—Use the handy trigger tool (found in quilt and fabric stores) that pushes nylon tags through all layers of the quilt. Start in center and work randomly toward outside edges. Place tags about 4" apart. You can sew right over the tags and then easily remove them by cutting them off with a pair of scissors.

Spray or heat-set basting—Use one of the spray adhesives currently on the market, following manufacturer's directions.

Fusible iron-on batting—The Gold-Fuse by Mountain Mist is a wonderful new way to hold the quilt layers together without using other time-consuming methods of basting.

Machine Quilting

If you have never used a sewing machine for quilting, you might want to read more about the technique. *Learn to Machine Quilt in Just One Weekend* (ASN #4186), by Marti Michell, is an excellent introduction to machine quilting.

This book is available at your local quilt or fabric store, or write the publisher for a list of sources.

You do not need a special machine for quilting. Just make sure your machine is oiled and in good working condition. An even-feed foot is a good investment if you are going to machine quilt, since it is designed to feed the top and bottom layers of the quilt through the machine evenly. It prevents pleats and puckers from forming as you machine quilt. Use fine transparent nylon thread in the top and regular sewing thread in the bobbin.

To quilt in the ditch of a seam (this is actually stitching in the space between two pieces of fabric that have been sewn together), use your fingers to pull blocks or pieces apart slightly and machine-stitch right between the two pieces. Try to keep stitching to the side of the seam that does not have the bulk of the seam allowance under it. When you have finished stitching, the quilting will be practically hidden in the seam.

Free-form machine quilting is done with a darning foot and the feed dogs down on your sewing machine. It can be used to quilt around a design or to quilt a motif. Free-form machine quilting takes practice to master because you are controlling the movement of the quilt under the needle, rather than the machine moving the quilt. With free-form machine quilting, you can quilt in any direction: up and down, side to side and even in circles, without pivoting the quilt around the needle. Practice first before doing free-form machine quilting on your quilt.

Attaching the Binding
Continuous Binding
Trim backing and batting even with quilt top. Cut enough 2½"-wide (or desired-width) strips to go around all four sides of the quilt, plus 6". Join strips end to end with diagonal seams; trim corners, **Fig 16**.

Fig 16

Press seams open. Cut one end of strip at a 45-degree angle, then press under ¼", **Fig 17**.

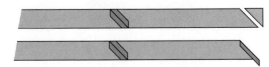

Fig 17

Press entire strip in half lengthwise, wrong sides together, **Fig 18**.

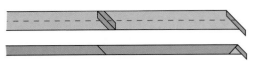

Fig 18

On right side of quilt, position binding in middle of one side, aligning raw edges. Sew binding to quilt using ¼" seam allowance, beginning about an inch below folded end of binding, **Fig 19**.

Fig 19

At corner, stop ¼" from edge of quilt and backstitch. Fold binding back on itself so fold is on quilt edge and sewn edges are aligned with adjacent side of quilt, **Fig 20**. Begin sewing at quilt edge.

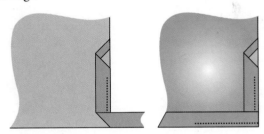

Fig 20

Continue in same manner around remaining sides of quilt. To finish, stop about 2" away from starting point. Trim excess binding, then tuck inside folded end, **Fig 21**. Finish line of stitching.

Fig 21

Fold binding to back of quilt so seam line is covered; blind-stitch in place.

The Finishing Touch
After your quilt is finished, always sign and date it. A label can be cross-stitched, embroidered or even written with a permanent marking pen. To make decorative labels in a hurry, *Iron-on Transfers for Quilt Labels* (ASN #4188) and *Foundation-Pieced Quilt Labels* (ASN #4196), provide many patterns for fun and unique quilt labels. Hand-stitch to back of quilt.

Floating Stars

Approximate Size: 52" x 61"

Materials

⅝ yd off-white star print (A)
⅜ yd off-white snowflake print (B)
⅜ yd dk green print (C)
¼ yd med green print (D)
¼ yd lt green print (E)
⅜ yd dk red print (F)
¼ yd med red print (G)
¼ yd lt red print (H)
¼ yd dk gold print (I)
⅛ yd med gold print (J)
⅛ yd lt gold print (K)
½ yd border 1 print
1⅛ yd border 2 print
3⅛ yds backing
⅝ yd binding
Batting

Cutting Requirements

Cut 4"-wide strips, then cut squares:
  5 strips cut into 49 squares, off-white star print (A)
  3 strips cut into 26 squares, dk green print (C)
  2 strips cut into 12 squares, med green print (D)
  2 strips cut into 12 squares, lt green print (E)
  3 strips cut into 26 squares, dk red print (F)
  2 strips cut into 12 squares, med red print (G)
  2 strips cut into 12 squares, lt red print (H)
  2 strips cut into 17 squares, dk gold print (I)
  1 strip cut into 6 squares, med gold print (J)
  1 strip cut into 6 squares, lt gold print (K)
Cut 3½"-wide strips, then cut squares:
  3 strips cut into 30 squares, off-white snowflake print (B)
Cut 5 – 2"-wide strips, border 1 print
Cut 6 – 5½"-wide strips, border 2 print
Cut 4 – 5½" squares, border 1 print
Cut 6 – 2½"-wide strips, binding

Instructions

1. Cut squares diagonally in half, **Fig 1**.

Fig 1

2. Place an A triangle right sides together with a C triangle; sew to complete triangle square. Chain-piece pairs of triangles in the following amounts, **Fig 2.**

A C	C E	D E	D C
make 36	make 8	make 16	make 8

A F	F G	H G	H F
make 36	make 8	make 16	make 8

I A	I J	K J	K I
make 26	make 4	make 8	make 4

Fig 2

3. Press triangle squares open with seams toward darker fabric and trim squares to 3½" square.

4. Place triangle squares and B squares according to quilt layout (or photo). Sew together in pairs, then sew pairs together, **Fig 3**. Continue sewing until quilt top is completed, **Fig 4**.

5. Add first border referring to Adding Borders, page 4. For second border, measure length and width of quilt. Cut two border strips for each measurement. Sew lengthwise strips to sides of quilt; press seams toward border.

Sew a 5½" border 1 print square to each end of remaining border strips. Sew to top and bottom of quilt. Press seams toward border.

6. Finish quilt referring to Finishing your Quilt, page 4.

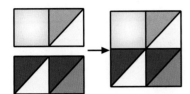

Fig 3

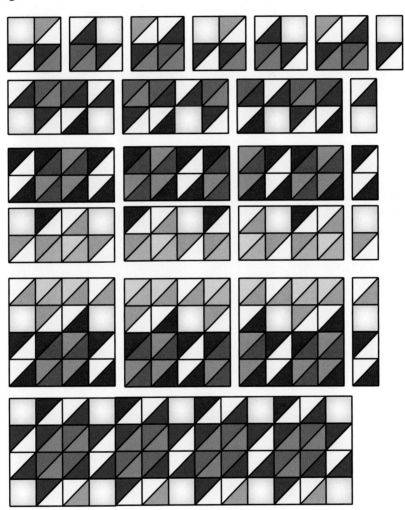

Fig 4

Pinwheel Trip

Approximate Size: 67" x 83"

Materials
1⅛ yds med peach (A)
1¼ yds lt peach (B)
⅞ yd turquoise (C)
1¼ yds lt purple (D)
⅝ yd dk purple (E)
½ yd border 1 print
1⅛ yds border 2 print
4¾ yds backing
⅝ yd binding
Batting

Cutting Requirements
Cut 5"-wide strips, then cut squares:
  7 strips cut into 54 squares, med peach (A)
  8 strips cut into 62 squares, lt peach (B)
  6 strips cut into 44 squares, turquoise (C)
  8 strips cut into 64 squares, lt purple (D)
  4 strips cut into 28 squares, dk purple (E)
Cut 7 – 2"-wide strips, border 1 print
Cut 7 – 4½"-wide strips, border 2 print
Cut 8 – 2½"-wide strips, binding

Instructions
1. Cut squares diagonally in half, **Fig 1**.

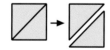

Fig 1

2. Place an A triangle right sides together with a B triangle; sew to complete triangle square. Chain-piece pairs of triangles in the following amounts, **Fig 2**.

 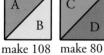
make 108   make 80   make 48   make 8   make 8

Fig 2

3. Press triangle squares open with seams toward darker fabric and trim squares to 4½" square.

4. Place triangle squares referring to photograph. Sew together in pairs, then sew pairs together, **Fig 3**. Continue sewing until quilt top is completed, **Fig 4**.

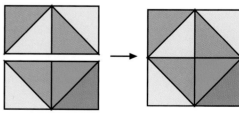

Fig 3

5. Add border referring to Adding Borders, page 4.

6. Finish quilt referring to Finishing your Quilt, page 4.

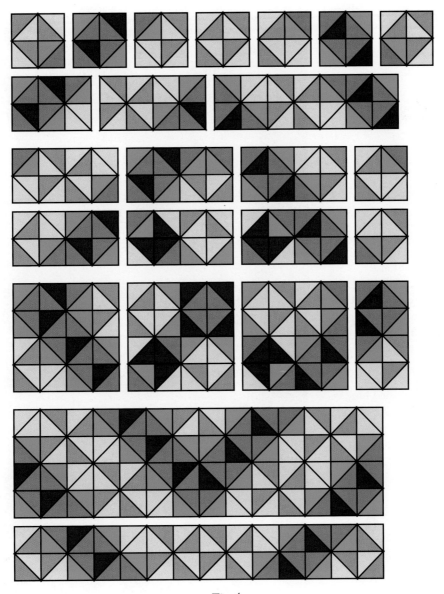

Fig 4

Patriotic Ripple

Approximate Size: 64" x 79"

Materials

⅝ yd dk red (A)
1 yd med red (B)
⅝ yd lt red (C)
½ yd white (D)
⅞ yd very lt blue (E)
⅞ yd lt blue (F)
⅞ yd med blue (G)
½ yd dk blue (H)
1¾ yds border print
4 yds backing
⅝ yd binding
Batting

Cutting Requirements

Cut 6"-wide strips, then cut squares:
  3 strips cut into 13 squares, dk red (A)
  5 strips cut into 25 squares, med red (B)
  3 strips cut into 13 squares, lt red (C)
  2 strips cut into 10 squares, white (D)
  4 strips cut into 20 squares, very lt blue (E)
  4 strips cut into 20 squares, lt blue (F)
  4 strips cut into 20 squares, med blue (G)
  2 strips cut into 10 squares, dk blue (H)
Cut 7 – 7½"-wide strips, border print
Cut 8 – 2½"-wide strips, binding

Instructions

1. Cut squares diagonally in half, **Fig 1**.

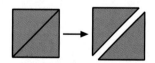

Fig 1

2. Place an A triangle right sides together with a B triangle; sew to complete triangle square. Chain-piece pairs of triangles in the following amounts, **Fig 2**.

3. Press triangle squares open with seams toward darker fabric and trim squares to 5½" square.

4. Place triangle squares referring to photograph. Sew together in pairs, then sew pairs together, **Fig 3**. Continue sewing until quilt top is completed, **Fig 4**.

5. Add border referring to Adding Borders, page 4.

6. Finish quilt referring to Finishing your Quilt, page 4.

make 15

make 15

make 10

make 10

make 10   make 20   make 20

make 10   make 10   make 10

Fig 2

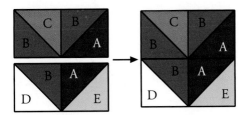

Fig 3

Fig 4

Rainbow Ripple

Approximate Size: 74" x 84"

Materials
⅝ yd red (A)
⅝ yd purple (B)
⅝ yd blue (C)
⅝ yd green (D)
⅝ yd yellow (E)
⅝ yd orange (F)
1⅜ yds black (G)
1⅜ yds dk gray (H)
¾ yds border 1 print
2¼ yds border 2 print (includes binding)
4⅞ yds backing
Batting

Cutting Requirements
Cut 6"-wide strips, then cut squares:
   3 strips cut into 14 squares, red (A)
   3 strips cut into 14 squares, purple (B)
   3 strips cut into 14 squares, blue (C)
   3 strips cut into 14 squares, green (D)
   3 strips cut into 14 squares, yellow (E)
   3 strips cut into 14 squares, orange (F)
   7 strips cut into 42 squares, black (G)
   7 strips cut into 42 squares, dk gray (H)
Cut 8 – 2½"-wide strips, border 1 print
Cut 8 – 5½"-wide strips, border 2 print
Cut 8 – 2½"-wide strips, binding

Instructions

1. Cut squares diagonally in half, **Fig 1**.

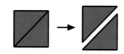

Fig 1

2. Place an A triangle right sides together with a G triangle; sew to complete triangle square. Chain-piece pairs of triangles in the following amounts, **Fig 2**.

3. Press triangle squares open with seams toward darker fabric and trim squares to 5½".

make 14 make 14 make 14 make 14

make 14 make 14 make 14 make 14

make 14 make 14 make 14 make 14

Fig 2

4. Sew two A/G triangle squares together; sew two A/H triangle squares; sew pairs together, **Fig 3**. Repeat for seven red blocks.

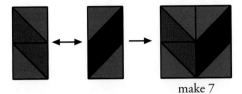

make 7

Fig 3

5. Repeat step 4 with purple and blue triangle squares, **Fig 4**.

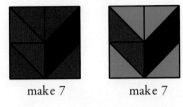

make 7   make 7

Fig 4

6. For green, yellow and orange triangle squares, make six blocks and two half-blocks in each color, **Fig 5**.

7. Place blocks and half-blocks referring to **Fig 6**.

8. Add border referring to Adding Borders, page 4.

9. Finish quilt referring to Finishing your Quilt, page 4.

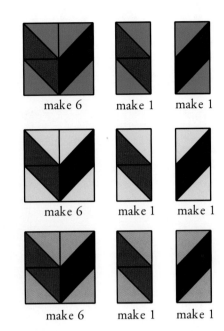

make 6   make 1   make 1

make 6   make 1   make 1

make 6   make 1   make 1

Fig 5

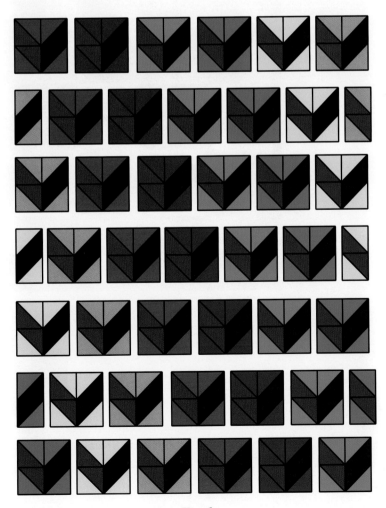

Fig 6

Trip Around the World

Approximate Size: 73" x 93"

Materials

1⅝ yds black print (A)
⅞ yd dk red (B)
⅞ yd lt red (C)
⅞ yd lt green (D)
⅞ yd dk green (E)
⅞ yd dk blue (F)
⅞ yd lt blue (G)
⅝ yd border print 1
1⅜ yds border print 2
5¼ yds backing
¾ yd binding
Batting

Cutting Requirements

Cut 6"-wide strips, then cut squares:
    8 strips cut into 48 squares, black
      print (A)
    2 strips cut into 8 squares,
      dk red (B)
    2 strips cut into 8 squares,
      lt red (C)
    2 strips cut into 8 squares,
      lt green (D)
    2 strips cut into 8 squares,
      dk green (E)
    2 strips cut into 8 squares,
      dk blue (F)
    2 strips cut into 9 squares,
      lt blue (G)
Cut 5½"-wide strips, then cut squares:
    2 strips cut into 16 squares,
      dk red (B)
    2 strips cut into 16 squares,
      lt red (C)
    2 strips cut into 16 squares,
      lt green (D)
    2 strips cut into 16 squares,
      dk green (E)
    2 strips cut into 16 squares,
      dk blue (F)
    2 strips cut into 16 squares, lt blue (G)
Cut 8 – 2"-wide strips, border print 1
Cut 8 – 5½"-wide strips, border print 2
Cut 9 – 2½"-wide strips, binding

Instructions

1. Cut 6" squares diagonally in half, **Fig 1**. *Note: Do not cut the 5½" squares in half.*

2. Place an A triangle right sides together with a B triangle;

Fig 1

sew to complete triangle square. Chain-piece pairs of triangles in the following amounts, **Fig 2** (on next page).

3. Press triangle squares open with seams toward darker fabric and trim squares to 5½" square.

Note: *This quilt is made in four sections. The first and fourth are* *the same and the second and third are the same, **Fig 3**; you will need to rotate sections 3 and 4 before sewing to 1 and 2.*

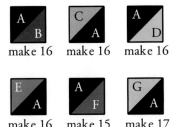

A B	C A	A D
make 16	make 16	make 16

E A	A F	G A
make 16	make 15	make 17

Fig 2

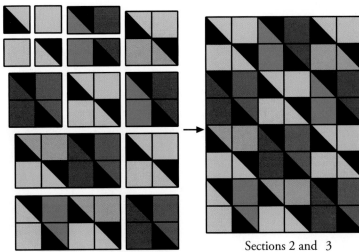

Sections 2 and 3

Fig 5

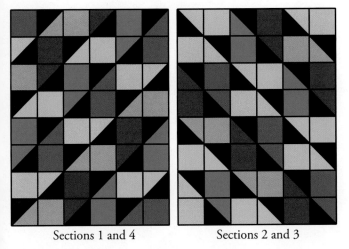

Sections 1 and 4   Sections 2 and 3

Fig 3

4. Place 5½" squares and triangle squares for section 1 according to **Fig 4**. Sew in pairs, then sew pairs together. Continue sewing to complete two sections.

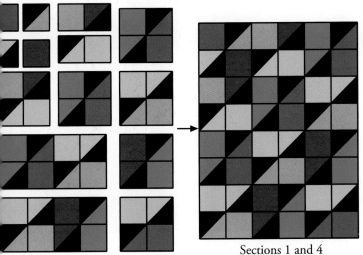

Sections 1 and 4

Fig 4

5. Place 5½" squares and triangle squares for section 2 according to **Fig 5**. Sew in pairs, then sew pairs together. Continue sewing to complete two sections.

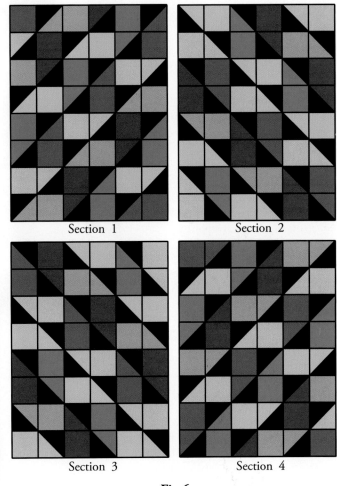

Section 1   Section 2

Section 3   Section 4

Fig 6

6. Sew sections 1 and 2 together; rotate sections 3 and 4 and sew together. Sew section 3/4 to section 1/2, **Fig 6**.

7. Add border referring to Adding Borders, page 4.

8. Finish quilt referring to Finishing your Quilt, page 4.

Small Trips

Approximate Size: 58" x 58"

Materials

1 yd cream dot print (A)
½ yd cream/cherry print (B)
¼ yd cream/star print (C)
⅜ yd burgundy/black print (D)
⅜ yd green/black print (E)
⅜ yd med green print (F)
⅜ yd dk green print (G)
⅜ yd med burgundy print (H)
⅜ yd dk burgundy print (I)
⅜ yd border 1 print
¾ yd border 2 print
3½ yds backing
½ yd binding
Batting

Cutting Requirements

Cut 4"-wide strips, then cut squares:
   8 strips cut into 72 squares, cream dot print (A)
   4 strips cut into 40 squares, cream/cherry print (B)
   2 strips cut into 16 squares, cream/star print (C)
   3 strips cut into 28 squares, burgundy/black (D)
   3 strips cut into 28 squares, green/black (E)
   1 strip cut into 6 squares, med green (F)
   1 strip cut into 6 squares, dk green (G)
   1 strip cut into 6 squares, med burgundy (H)
   1 strip cut into 6 squares, dk burgundy (I)
Cut 3½"-wide strips, then cut squares:
   2 strips cut into 12 squares, med green (F)
   2 strips cut into 12 squares, dk green (G)
   2 strips cut into 12 squares, med burgundy (H)
   2 strips cut into 12 squares, dk burgundy (I)
Cut 5 – 2"-wide strips, border 1 print
Cut 6 – 4"-wide strips, border 2 print
Cut 6 – 2½"-wide strips, binding

Instructions

1. Cut 4" squares diagonally in half, **Fig 1**. *Note: Do not cut the 3½" squares in half.*

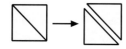

Fig 1

2. Place an A triangle right sides together with a B triangle; sew to complete triangle square. Chain-piece pairs of triangles in the following amounts, **Fig 2**.

make 64   make 16   make 16

make 32   make 32   make 12

make 12   make 12   make 12

Fig 2

3. Press triangle squares open with seams toward darker fabric and trim squares to 3½" square.

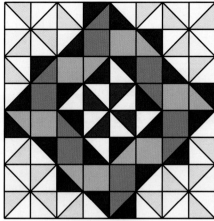

Sections 1 and 4

Sections 2 and 3

Fig 3

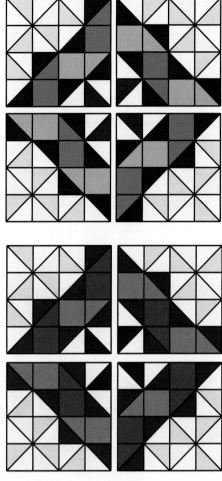

Fig 4

Note: *This quilt is made up of four sections. Sections 1 and 4 are the same as well as sections 2 and 3,* **Fig 3**. *Within each section are four smaller sections with the first and fourth being the same as well as the second and third,* **Fig 4**.

4. For section 1, place triangle squares and 3½" squares according to **Fig 5**.

5. Sew together in pairs, then sew pairs together, Continue sewing in pairs until section is complete.

6. Repeat steps 4 and 5 for section 4.

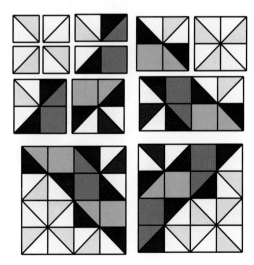

Fig 5

7. Repeat steps 4–6 for sections 2 and 3, replacing med and dk green with med and dk burgundy and the burgundy/black print with the green/black print, **Fig 6**.

8. Sew sections together in pairs, then sew pairs together, **Fig 7**.

9. Add border referring to Adding Borders, page 4.

10. Finish quilt referring to Finishing your Quilt, page 4.

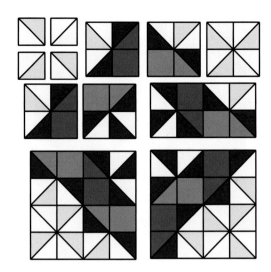

Fig 6

Fig 7

Hidden Stars

Approximate Size: 72" x 88"

Materials

1⅛ yds white (A)
⅝ yd dk pink (B)
⅜ yd lt pink (C)
½ yd dk yellow (D)
⅜ yd lt yellow (E)
¾ yd dk green (F)
⅜ yd lt green (G)
⅝ yd dk peach (H)
⅜ yd lt peach (I)
½ yd dk purple (J)
⅜ yd lt purple (K)
½ yd dk blue (L)
¼ yd lt blue (M)
⅝ yd border 1 print
1⅝ yds border 2 print
⅝ yd binding
5 yds backing
Batting

Note: If making a pieced border as shown on project, add ¼ yd to fabrics B through M. Cut 2 – 2½"-wide strips each fabric.

Cutting Requirements

Cut 5"-wide strips, then cut squares:

    7 strips cut into 51 squares, white (A)

    4 strips cut into 25 squares, dk pink (B)

    2 strips cut into 7 squares, lt pink (C)

    3 strips cut into 21 squares, dk yellow (D)

    2 strips cut into 7 squares, lt yellow (E)

    5 strips cut into 36 squares, dk green (F)

    2 strips cut into 13 squares, lt green (G)

    4 strips cut into 28 squares, dk peach (H)

    2 strips cut into 9 squares, lt peach (I)

    3 strips cut into 23 squares, dk purple (J)

    2 strips cut into 8 squares, lt purple (K)

    3 strips cut into 19 squares, dk blue (L)

    1 strip cut into 6 squares, lt blue (M)

Cut 7 – 2½"-wide strips, border 1 print

Cut 8 – 6½"-wide strips, border 2 print

Cut 8 – 2½"-wide strips, binding

Note: Cut 2 – 2½"-wide strips each, fabrics B through M if making pieced border.

Instructions

1. Cut squares diagonally in half, **Fig 1**.

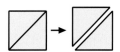

Fig 1

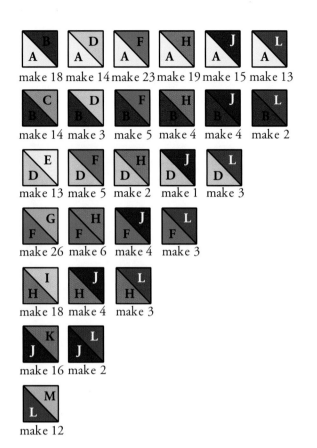

make 18 make 14 make 23 make 19 make 15 make 13

make 14 make 3 make 5 make 4 make 4 make 2

make 13 make 5 make 2 make 1 make 3

make 26 make 6 make 4 make 3

make 18 make 4 make 3

make 16 make 2

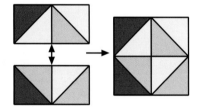

make 12

Fig 2

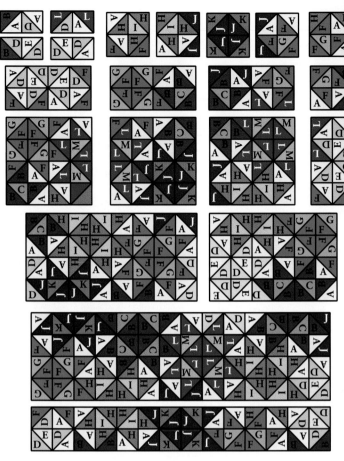

Fig 4

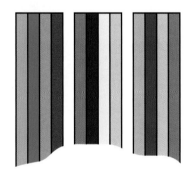

Fig 5

Fig 3

2. Place an A triangle right sides together with a B triangle; sew to complete triangle square. Chain-piece pairs of triangles in the following amounts, **Fig 2**.

3. Press triangle squares open with seams toward darker fabric and trim squares to 4½" square.

4. Place triangle squares referring to photograph. Sew together in pairs, then sew pairs together, **Fig 3**. Continue sewing until quilt top is completed, **Fig 4**.

5. Add border referring to Adding Borders, page 4. For pieced border, sew strips randomly in sets of four, **Fig 5**. You will need six strip sets. Press seams to one side.

6. Cut strip sets at 6½" intervals, **Fig 6**.

7. Sew pieced strips end to end until necessary length is achieved, **Fig 7**: 44 individual strips for each side and 36 for top and bottom.

8. Starting with one side, place pieced strip with top edge of fourth strip even with top edge of quilt; pin strip to quilt top. There should be three strips left below bottom edge of quilt, **Fig 8**. Sew strip to quilt beginning ¼" from edges; backstitch at each end. Be sure not to catch loose ends of pieced strip in sewing. Repeat for remaining three sides.

9. To miter corners, fold quilt in half diagonally; border ends will be right sides together, extending past quilt. Draw diagonal line on border even with diagonal fold of quilt, **Fig 9**. Sew along drawn line. Check miter to see if it is even, then trim corner ¼" from seam. Repeat at remaining corners.

10. Finish quilt referring to Finishing your Quilt, page 4.

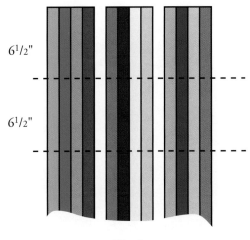

6¹/₂"

6¹/₂"

Fig 6

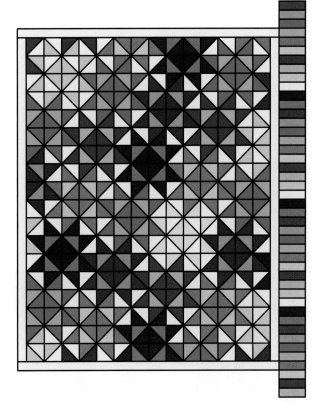

Fig 8

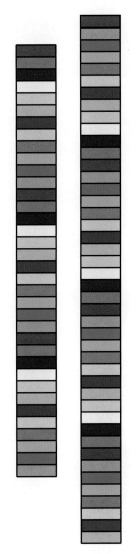

Fig 7

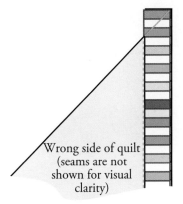

Wrong side of quilt (seams are not shown for visual clarity)

Fig 9

Hearts & Tulips

Approximate Size:
47" x 55"

Materials
⅞ yd very lt pink (A)
1 yd very lt green (B)
⅜ yd dk green (C)
⅝ yd dk pink (D)
⅜ yd med pink (E)

¼ yd border 1 print
⅞ yd border 2 print
3 yds backing
½ yd binding
Batting

Cutting Requirements
Cut 5¼"-wide strips, then
    cut squares:

5 strips cut into 29
    squares, very lt pink (A)
6 strips cut into 32
    squares, very lt green (B)
2 strips cut into 12
    squares, dk green (C)
3 strips cut into 17
    squares, dk pink (D)

2 strips cut into eleven
    squares, med pink (E)
Cut 5 – 1½"-wide strips,
    border 1 print
Cut 6 – 5"-wide strips,
    border 2 print
Cut 6 – 2½"-wide strips,
    binding

Instructions

1. Cut squares diagonally in quarters, **Fig 1**.

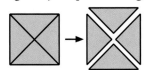

Fig 1

2. Place an A triangle right sides together with a B triangle; sew to complete pieced triangle. Chain-piece pairs of triangles in the following amounts, **Fig 2**.

B / A 1=A/B make 70	D / A 5=A/D make 16	D / E 9=E/D make 2
C / A 2=A/C make 16	B / E 6=E/B make 12	E / D 10=D/E make 2
B / C 3=C/B make 28	E / A 7=A/E make 12	D / D 11=D/D make 15
C / B 4=B/C make 2	B / D 8=D/B make 14	E / E 12=E/E make 7
		D / C 13=C/D make 2

Fig 2

3. Press triangles open with seams toward darker fabric.

4. Place pieced triangles according to **Fig 3**.

5. Sew pieced triangles in pairs to complete pieced squares, **Fig 4**. Be sure to keep pieced squares in the same order throughout.

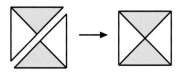

Fig 4

6. Trim squares to 5½" square.

7. Sew pieced squares together in sections, **Fig 5**, then sew sections together until quilt top is completed.

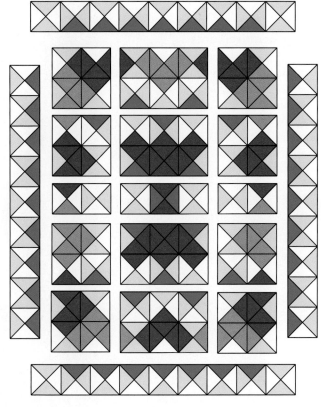

Fig 5

8. Add borders referring to Adding Borders, page 4.

9. Finish quilt referring to Finishing your Quilt, page 4.

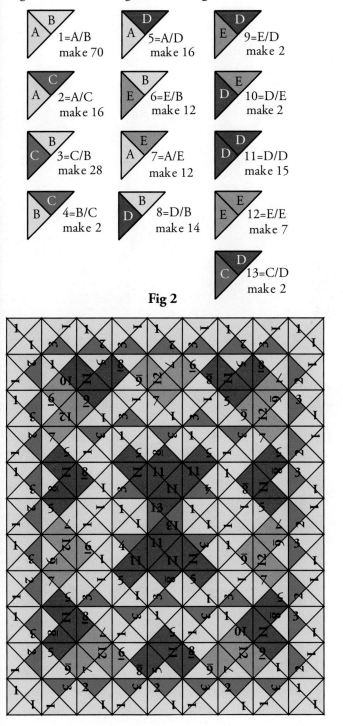

Fig 3

Pinwheel Chain

Approximate Size: 60" x 76"

Materials

1 yd white (A)
1⅜ yds lt yellow (B)
¾ yd black print (C)
¾ yd pink print (D)
½ yd border 1 print
1 yd border 2 print
3½ yds backing
⅝ yd binding
Batting

Cutting Requirements

Cut 5"-wide strips, then cut squares:
   6 strips cut into 48 squares, white (A)
   9 strips cut into 72 squares, lt yellow (B)
   5 strips cut into 36 squares, black print (C)
   5 strips cut into 36 squares, pink print (D)
Cut 7 – 2"-wide strips, border 1 print
Cut 7 – 5"-wide strips, border 2 print
Cut 7 – 2½"-wide strips, binding

Instructions

1. Cut squares diagonally in half, **Fig 1**.

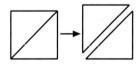

Fig 1

2. Place an A triangle right sides together with a B triangle; sew to complete triangle square. Chain-piece pairs of triangles in the following amounts, **Fig 2**.

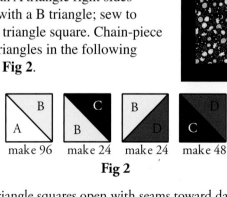

make 96   make 24   make 24   make 48

Fig 2

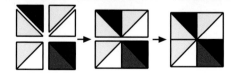

Fig 3

3. Press triangle squares open with seams toward darker fabric and trim squares to 4½" square.

4. Place triangle squares referring to photo. Sew together in pairs, then sew pairs together, **Fig 3**.

5. Continue sewing until quilt top is completed, **Fig 4**.

6. Add border referring to Adding Borders, page 4.

7. Finish quilt referring to Finishing your Quilt, page 4.

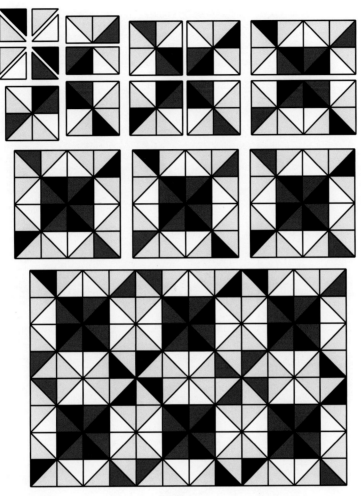

Fig 4

Chain Link

Approximate Size: 63" x 73"

Materials

⅝ yd very lt purple (A)
⅝ yd very lt green (B)
⅝ yd white (C)
⅞ yd dk turquoise 1 (D)
⅞ yd dk turquoise 2 (E)
⅞ yd dk purple 1 (F)
⅞ yd dk purple 2 (G)
½ yd border 1 print
1¼ yds border 2 print
3¾ yds backing
⅝ yd binding
Batting

Cutting Requirements

Cut 6¼"-wide strips, then cut squares:

    3 strips cut into 15 squares, very lt purple (A)

    3 strips cut into 15 squares, very lt green (B)

    3 strips cut into 15 squares, white (C)

    4 strips cut into 19 squares, dk turquoise 1 (D)

    4 strips cut into 19 squares, dk turquoise 2 (E)

    4 strips cut into 19 squares, dk purple 1 (F)

    4 strips cut into 19 squares, dk purple 2 (G)

Cut 6 – 2"-wide strips, border 1 print

Cut 7 – 5½"-wide strips, border 2 print

Cut 8 – 2½"-wide strips, binding

Instructions

1. Cut squares diagonally in quarters, **Fig 1**.

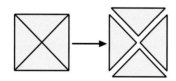

Fig 1

2. Place an A triangle right sides together with a B triangle; sew to complete pieced triangle, **Fig 2**. Chain-piece pairs of triangles in the following amounts, **Fig 3**.

3. Press triangles open with seams toward darker fabric.

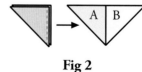

Fig 2

4. Sew pairs of triangles to complete pieced squares, **Fig 4**. Trim squares to 5½" square.

5. Place pieced squares according to **Fig 5**. Sew together in pairs, then sew pairs together. Continue sewing until quilt top is completed.

6. Add borders referring to Adding Borders, page 4.

7. Finish quilt referring to Finishing your Quilt, page 4.

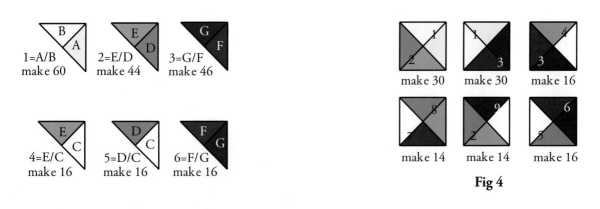

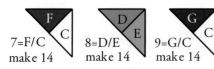

1=A/B make 60   2=E/D make 44   3=G/F make 46

4=E/C make 16   5=D/C make 16   6=F/G make 16

7=F/C make 14   8=D/E make 14   9=G/C make 14

Fig 3

make 30   make 30   make 16

make 14   make 14   make 16

Fig 4

Fig 5

Twirling Pinwheels

Approximate Size: 64" x 79"

Materials

1⅛ yds white (A)
1⅛ yds off-white print (B)
⅝ yd pink print 1 (C)
⅝ yd pink print 2 (D)
⅝ yd blue print 1 (E)
⅝ yd blue print 2 (F)
⅜ yd black print (G)
½ yd border 1 print
1¼ yd border 2 print
1¼ yds border 3 print
3¾ yds backing
⅝ yd binding
Batting

Cutting Requirements

Cut 6¼"-wide strips, then cut squares:
    6 strips cut into 32 squares, white (A)
    6 strips cut into 32 squares, off-white (B)
    3 strips cut into 14 squares, pink print 1 (C)
    3 strips cut into 14 squares, pink print 2 (D)
    3 strips cut into 14 squares, blue print 1 (E)
    3 strips cut into 14 squares, blue print 2 (F)
    2 strips cut into 12 squares, black print (G)
Cut 7 – 2"-wide strips, border 1 print
Cut 7 – 5½"-wide strips, border 2 print
Cut 8 – 2½"-wide strips, binding

Instructions

1. Cut squares diagonally in quarters, **Fig 1**.

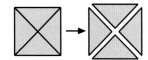

Fig 1

2. Place an A triangle right sides together with a B triangle; sew to complete pieced triangle. Chain-piece pairs of triangles in the following amounts, **Fig 2**.

3. Press triangle open with seams toward darker fabric.

4. Sew pairs of triangles to complete pieced squares, **Fig 3**.

5. Trim squares to 5½" square.

6. Place pieced squares referring to photograph. Sew together in pairs, then sew pairs together, **Fig 4**. Continue sewing until quilt top is completed.

7. Add borders referring to Adding Borders, page 4.

8. Finish quilt referring to Finishing your Quilt, page 4.

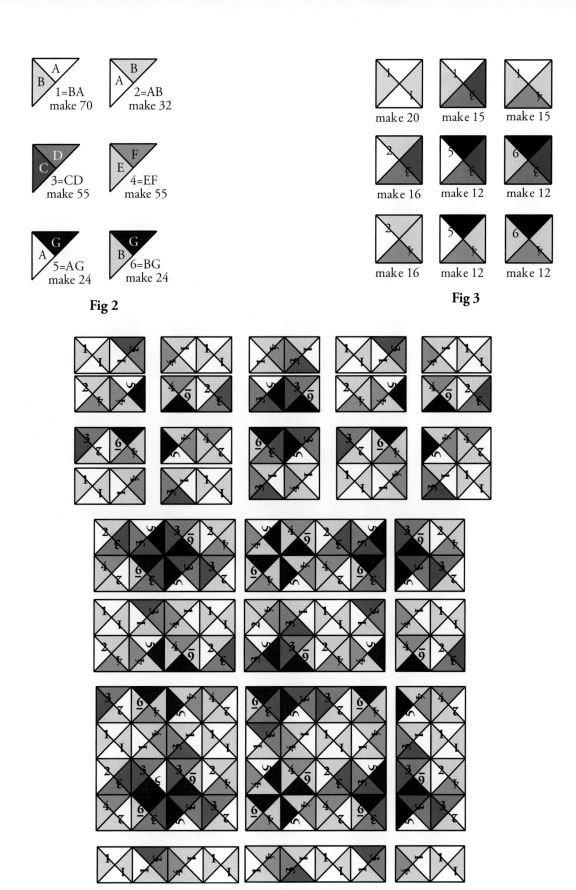

Fig 2

1=BA make 70
2=AB make 32
3=CD make 55
4=EF make 55
5=AG make 24
6=BG make 24

Fig 3

make 20   make 15   make 15
make 16   make 12   make 12
make 16   make 12   make 12

Fig 4

Starry Night

Approximate Size: 72" x 82"

Materials

1¾ yds dk blue sparkle (A)
1⅛ yds dk blue (B)
⅝ yd med blue (C)
1¼ yds lt blue (D)
¼ yd med green (E)
¼ yd lt green (F)
¼ yd med yellow (G)
¼ yd lt yellow (H)
¼ yd med pink (I)
¼ yd lt pink (J)
¼ yd med purple (K)
¼ yd lt purple (L)
¼ yd med aqua (M)
¼ yd lt aqua (N)
⅝ yd inner border print
1 yd outer border print
5 yds backing
⅝ yd binding
Batting

Cutting Requirements

Cut 6¼"-wide strips, then cut squares:
    9 strips cut into 50 squares, dk blue
      sparkle (A)
    6 strips cut into 35 squares,
      dk blue (B)
    3 strips cut into 16 squares,
      med blue (C)
    6 strips cut into 31 squares,
      lt blue (D)
    1 strip cut into 3 squares,
      med green (E)
    1 strip cut into 5 squares,
      lt green (F)
    1 strip cut into 3 squares, med yellow (G)
    1 strip cut into 5 squares, lt yellow (H)
    1 strip cut into 3 squares, med pink (I)
    1 strip cut into 5 squares, lt pink (J)
    1 strip cut into 3 squares, med purple (K)
    1 strip cut into 5 squares, lt purple (L)
    1 strip cut into 3 squares, med aqua (M)
    1 strip cut into 5 squares, lt aqua (N)
Cut 6 – 3"-wide strips, inner border print
Cut 8 – 4"-wide strips, outer border print
Cut 8 – 2½"-wide strips, binding

Instructions

1. Cut squares diagonally in quarters, **Fig 1**.

2. Place an A triangle right sides together with a B triangle;

Fig 1

sew to complete pieced triangle. Chain-piece pairs of triangles in the following amounts, **Fig 2**.

3. Press triangle open with seams toward darker fabric.

4. Sew pairs of triangles to complete pieced squares, **Fig 3**.

5. Trim squares to 5½" square.

6. Place all but 52 AD/CD pieced squares referring to photograph. Sew together in pairs, then sew pairs together, **Fig 4**. Continue sewing until quilt top is completed.

. Add first border referring to Adding Borders, page 4. For
econd border, sew together 13 AD/CD pieced squares for
ides and 13 for top and bottom, **Fig 5**. Sew to quilt top.
dd third border.

. Finish quilt referring to Finishing your Quilt, page 4.

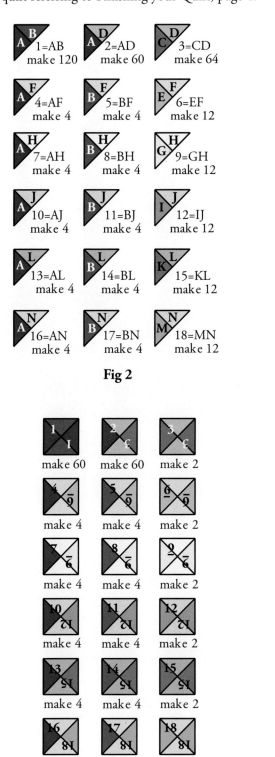

1=AB make 120
2=AD make 60
3=CD make 64
4=AF make 4
5=BF make 4
6=EF make 12
7=AH make 4
8=BH make 4
9=GH make 12
10=AJ make 4
11=BJ make 4
12=IJ make 12
13=AL make 4
14=BL make 4
15=KL make 12
16=AN make 4
17=BN make 4
18=MN make 12

Fig 2

1 make 60
2 make 60
3 make 2
4 make 4
5 make 4
6 make 2
7 make 4
8 make 4
9 make 2
10 make 4
11 make 4
12 make 2
13 make 4
14 make 4
15 make 2
16 make 4
17 make 4
18 make 2

Fig 3

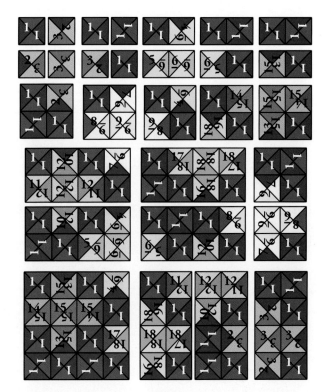

Fig 4

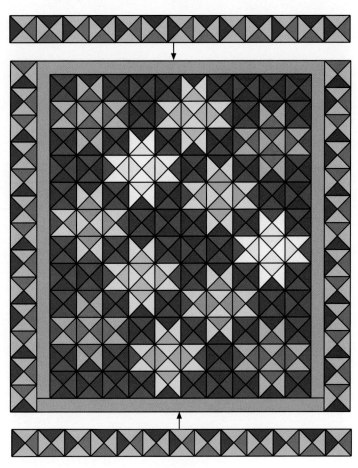

Fig 5

We wish to thank following companies who generously supplied products for our quilts:

Bernina® of America: Artista 180 sewing machine

Güterman: 100% cotton sewing thread

Stearns Technical Textile Company: Mountain Mist® White Rose 100% Cotton Batting

Pictured quilts were made by Sandy Anderson, Linda Causee, Rosie Gonzalez, Cheryl Gould, Ann Hogan, Questa Hogan, Faith Horsky, Sandy Hunter, Wendy Mathson, Sue Ragan, and Debby Sharp.

Quilts were machine quilted by Faith Horsky.

American
School of
Needlework®
excellence
in instruction

2420 Grand Avenue, Suite H
Vista, CA 92081
www.ASNpub.com
© 2004 American School of Needlework, Inc.

The full line of ASN products is carried by Annie's Attic catalog.
TOLL-FREE ORDER LINE or to request a free catalog (800) 582-6643
Customer Service (800) 282-6643, **Fax** (800) 882-6643
Visit www.AnniesAttic.com

ISBN: 1-59012-049-3   All rights reserved.   Printed in USA   4 5 6 7 8 9